Countries Around the World

Russia

Jilly Hunt

Heinemann Library
Chicago, Illinois

www.capstonepub.com
Visit our website to find out more information about Heinemann-Raintree books.

To order:

☎ Phone 888-454-2279

💻 Visit www.capstonepub.com to browse our catalog and order online.

Edited by Laura Knowles
Designed by Victoria Allen
Original illustrations © Capstone Global Library Ltd 2012
Illustrated by Oxford Designers and Illustrators
Picture research by Mica Brancic
Originated by Capstone Global Library Ltd 2012
Printed and bound in China by CTPS

15 14 13 12 11
10 9 8 7 6 5 4 3 2 1

Library of Congress Cataloging-in-Publication Data
Hunt, Jilly.
  Russia / Jilly Hunt.
    p. cm.—(Countries around the world)
  Includes bibliographical references and index.
  ISBN 978-1-4329-6110-7 (hbk.)—ISBN 978-1-4329-6136-7 (pbk.) 1. Russia (Federation)—Juvenile literature. 2. Russia—Juvenile literature. 3. Soviet Union—Juvenile literature. I. Title.
  DK510.23.H86 2012
  947—dc22   2011015438

Acknowledgments
We would like to thank the following for permission to reproduce photographs: © Corbis p. 7; Corbis pp. 9 (© Hulton-Deutsch Collection), 10 (© Hulton-Deutsch Collection), 11 (© Hulton-Deutsch Collection), 12 (© Bettmann), 13 (Sygma/© Rick Maiman), 17 (© Gerd Ludwig), 28 (epa/© Sergei Chirikov), 30 (Lebrecht Music & Arts/© Lebrecht Authors), 31 (© Hulton-Deutsch Collection); Getty Images pp. 6 (Taxi/FPG), 26 (National Geographic/ Gordon Wiltsie); iStockphoto pp. 8 (© Nadezhda Bolotina), 33 (© Emiko Taki); Shutterstock pp. 5 (© ArtComma); Shutterstock pp. 15 (© Milevshi), 19 (© Pichugin Dmitry), 20 (© Belizar), 24 (© Sergiy Dontsov), 27 (© Petro Feketa), 29 (© S. Borisov), 34 (© Krechet), 35 (© Liseykina), 36 (© Mikhail Markovskiy), 46 (© Angilla S.).

Cover photograph of Tsarskoye selo, formerly Pushkin imperial estate, in St. Petersburg, Russia, reproduced with permission of Shutterstock/© Dainis Derics.

We would like to thank Daniel Block and Dr. Mara Sukholutskaya for their invaluable help in the preparation of this book.

Every effort has been made to contact copyright holders of material reproduced in this book. Any omissions will be rectified in subsequent printings if notice is given to the publisher.

Contents

Some words are printed in bold, **like this**. You can find out what they mean by looking in the glossary.

Introducing Russia

What do you think of when you think of Russia? Russian dolls? Very cold winters? Siberia? The Cold War? **Communism**? Russia is a vast country with a fascinating history and a unique culture.

Russia is the largest country in the world. It has a great variety of landscapes and some impressive places. It has the deepest, oldest lake in the world; the longest border of any country; and the longest river and highest mountain in Europe.

Population

Over 140 million people live in Russia. Most of these are Russians. There are also more than 120 other **ethnic groups**, including Ukrainians, Bashkirs, Chuvashs, Uzbeks, Belarusians, Kazakhs, Azerbaijanis, and Tatars. Russia is a federation, which means that the country of Russia is made up of different regions and **republics** all under one government. Many of the ethnic groups are from these different regions or republics of Russia.

In the past many people lived in **rural** areas, but now almost three quarters of the population live in **urban** areas. Russia's capital city is Moscow, and other main cities include St. Petersburg, Novosibirsk, and Nizhny Novgorod.

A different alphabet

The Russian language uses the Cyrillic alphabet. This alphabet was developed by Greek **missionaries** who moved into Russia in the 980s CE. Russian is the official language of the country, but the different regions have their own languages, too.

How to say...

hello	*здра́вствуйте*	(zdrah-stvuy-tyeh)
goodbye	*досвидаія*	(da svee-da-nyah)

The Ural Mountains form the traditional divide between Europe and Asia.

History: Tsars and Revolutions

People have been living in Russia for a million years. Around 2,000 years ago, the **Slavic people** first settled in Russia. For centuries, Russia was ruled by a *tsar*, or **emperor**, who came from a family of rulers. The Russians view their first **dynasty** as having started in 862 CE, with the leader Rurik.

The Romanov dynasty

In 1613, Mikail Romanov was elected as ruler. This was the beginning of the Romanov Dynasty, which was to rule until 1917—just over 300 years! Russia became the largest **empire** in the world under the Romanov dynasty.

CATHERINE THE GREAT (1729–1796)

One of Russia's great rulers was Catherine the Great, who was only a Romanov by marriage. She was the wife of Peter III. People did not like Peter and his beliefs, and in July 1762 the army arrested him. Catherine became empress and took over the rule of the empire. She expanded Russia's territory even further.

Tsar Nicholas II was the last tsar to rule the Russian Empire. He is seen here with his family. The family was murdered by the **Bolsheviks** in July 1918. The location of their remains has been a mystery.

Russian Revolution

The last Romanov emperor was Nicholas II, who **abdicated** in 1917. He was forced to abdicate because of a series of defeats. Russia's defeat in the Russo-Japanese War of 1904–1905 led to the Russian Revolution of 1905. Following this revolution, Nicholas agreed to have a government, but he eventually took most of its power away. During World War I, Russia lost more battles. These defeats led to rioting and to the **imperial** household being overthrown by another revolution in 1917.

This photo shows a parade of Bolshevik soldiers in the streets of Moscow in 1917. The Bolsheviks began ruling Russia following the 1917 revolution.

Formation of the USSR

Nicholas II lost control of Russia, and the Bolshevik Party took over in 1917. This was a group of revolutionaries led by Vladimir Lenin. They established a communist government and withdrew Russia from World War I. They wanted to make society a fairer place. Under the *tsars*, the division of wealth was not equal. Some people were incredibly rich and other people were extremely poor. The communists believed that there should be a **communal** ownership of property.

In 1922 the communists formed a group of **republics**, called the **USSR** (Union of Soviet Socialist Republics). It became known as the Soviet Union. Russia was now called the Russian Federation, and was the largest of the republics. Other republics included Ukraine and Belorussia (now Belarus), and later Estonia, Latvia, Lithuania, and Uzbekistan.

Daily life

Life under the Bolsheviks remained tough. The three years of **civil war** that followed the end of the imperial family had exhausted Russia. Parts of the countryside had stopped sending food to the towns because **inflation** was so high that the money they got for it was not worth anything. In the cities, factories had to close because there were no **raw materials** to work with.

VLADIMIR ILYICH LENIN

(1870-1924)

Lenin was born as Vladimir Ilyich Ulyanov in Simbirsk, Russia, on April 22, 1870. He decided to change his name to Lenin in 1901. Lenin took over the control of Russia in 1917. Although Lenin was fighting the cause for peasants and workers, he had little contact with them and could be merciless toward them. There was a great deal of suffering during his rule. The violent tactics he used were known as the "**Red Terror**." After two years of illness, Lenin died on January 21, 1924, at age 53.

The rise of Stalin

After Lenin died in 1924, there was a power struggle between Leon Trotsky and Joseph Stalin. Stalin won and forced Trotsky to leave the Soviet Union in 1929. Stalin ruled as a **dictator** and made many changes. He set about **industrializing** the USSR. For example, he forced peasants to work as employees on **collective farms**. The wealthier farmers did not want collectivization to happen, so they resisted. The government seized their land and possessions. In 1932–1933, Stalin created a **famine** in Ukraine (part of the USSR) that killed between four and five million Ukrainian peasants.

JOSEPH STALIN
(1879-1953)

Stalin took control of the USSR in 1924, but he was worried that he would lose power. So he had a secret police force that he used to remove all his enemies. This period is known as the "Great Terror." Millions of people were killed. Estimates range from three million to more than ten million people.

Pact with Germany

Stalin was fearful of attack from **Nazi** Germany. Its leader, Adolf Hitler, wanted to destroy Soviet **communism**. However, in 1939, Stalin made a secret pact (promise) with Hitler that each country would not attack the other. This gave Stalin more time to build up his army. As a result of the pact, Hitler felt safe to invade Poland on September 1, 1939. This was the start of World War II.

After Hitler invaded Poland, Stalin invaded Finland and parts of eastern Europe. By 1941, Stalin and Hitler controlled most of Europe. In June 1941, Germany invaded the Soviet Union, breaking the secret pact between them. As a result, the Soviet Union joined the **allied forces**, led by the United States and Great Britain, to fight against Germany. The Soviet Union played a very important role in World War II, and Germany was finally defeated in 1945.

In the Soviet Union, World War II was known as the "Great Patriotic War." The Soviet Union suffered huge losses, with more than 20 million soldiers and civilians killed.

The start of the Cold War

World War II changed Europe. Before the war, Germany was the greatest military power in Europe, but it was now defeated. The Soviet Union had suffered great losses, but it still controlled almost all of eastern Europe. The Soviet Union set up communist governments in the countries it occupied. The United States and Great Britain had **democratic** governments and feared this rise in communism. This was the start of a long period of tension and competition between the United States and the Soviet Union known as the Cold War. They never fought each other directly, but they would support opposing armies in struggles throughout the world.

Joseph Stalin died in 1953 after 29 years in power, and the worst era in Soviet history came to an end. There was more calm within the Soviet Union now.

End of the Cold War and the Soviet Union

Developments in the Soviet Union and changes in its leadership after Stalin's death led to the end of the Cold War. In 1985, Mikhail Gorbachev became head of the Communist Party. He introduced new policies that encouraged reforms but weakened the strength of the Communist Party. Power began to move to the individual republics that made up the Soviet Union. By the end of 1989, the eastern European countries had broken free of the Soviet Union. By the end of 1991, the Soviet Union had come to an end, and Russia became an independent nation.

Daily life

The people of the Soviet Union were not able to speak freely against the government or help choose their leader. Gorbachev changed the rules of the Soviet government so that it allowed ordinary people to be involved in politics. He also allowed people to speak more freely and have access to more information.

Mikhail Gorbachev became general secretary of the Communist Party in 1985, and president in 1988. He resigned as president in December 1991, following the breakup of the USSR.

Regions and Resources: Biggest and Coldest

Russia is the world's largest country, with an area of 6,601,700 square miles (17,098,200 square kilometers). Russia is almost twice as big as the United States or China. Russia lies partly on the continent of Europe and partly on the continent of Asia. The Ural Mountains, which run north to south, form the traditional boundary between Europe and Asia.

Russia covers most of eastern Europe and the whole of northern Asia. Russia has the longest border of any country in the world! This map shows the main physical features of the country.

Land height:
- Over 6,550 feet
- Over 3,250 feet
- Over 1,300 feet
- Over 650 feet
- Above sea level
- Below sea level
- Country borders

0   750   1500 kilometers
0   500   1000 miles

N

Arctic Ocean

SWEDEN
Baltic Sea   FINLAND
POLAND   ESTONIA   Lake Ladoga
LATVIA
LITHUANIA   Lake Onega
BELARUS
■ Moscow
UKRAINE
Volga   Ural Mountains   Ob
Black Sea   Irtysh
Caucasus Mts.   Yenisey
▲ Mount Elbrus
GEORGIA
ARMENIA   KAZAKHSTAN
AZERBAIJAN   Aral
Caspian Sea   Sea
TURKMENISTAN
UZBEKISTAN
IRAN

Arctic Circle
RUSSIA   SIBERIA   Lena
Amur
Lake
Baikal
MONGOLIA
CHINA
NORTH
KOREA
SOUTH
KOREA

Kamchatka
Peninsula
Kuril
Islands
JAPAN

Pacific Ocean

There are a number of active volcanoes on the Kamachatka Peninsula, in the far east of Russia.

Landscape

Around the Arctic Ocean there are vast frozen plains known as tundra. The region of Siberia in northern Russia is mostly taiga, which are huge evergreen forests. West of the Ural Mountains it is mostly flat or **undulating** land. To the southeast, the land rises toward to the Caucasus Mountains. This is where Mount Elbrus is found—Russia's highest point, at 18,510 feet (5,642 meters). The Kamchatka Peninsula in the far east of Russia and the Kuril islands contain many active volcanoes.

Climate

The climate in Russia varies. In much of Russia it is continental. This means that summers can be hot and humid (damp) and winters are cold. However, the Arctic tundra and Siberia have extremely cold winters. Russia has the lowest temperature ever recorded outside Antactica of -96 degrees Fahrenheit (-71 degrees Celsius). This was recorded in the Siberian city of Oymyakon in 1926.

Agriculture

The climate in much of Russia is so harsh that only a relatively small area of land is farmed. Most of the farmland is used for growing crops, with the rest used for grazing animals. On the grasslands, crops such as wheat, barley, rye, and oats are grown. Beef cattle and pigs are raised. Millet and melons are grown along the lower Volga River.

This map shows the population density of the various regions in Russia. Although only 25 percent of the country lies west of the Ural Mountains, it is home to 80 percent of the population.

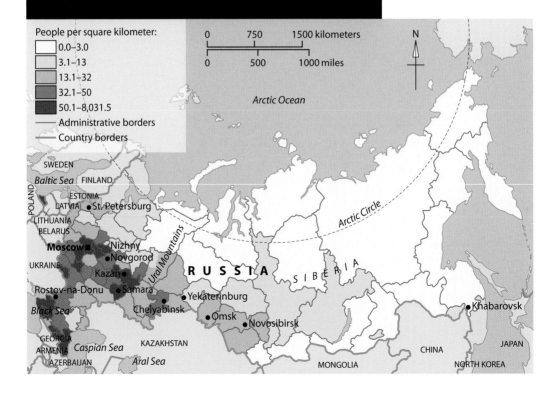

People per square kilometer:
- 0.0–3.0
- 3.1–13
- 13.1–32
- 32.1–50
- 50.1–8,031.5
- —— Administrative borders
- —— Country borders

0   750   1500 kilometers
0   500   1000 miles

N

Arctic Ocean

SWEDEN
Baltic Sea FINLAND
POLAND
ESTONIA
LATVIA ●St. Petersburg
LITHUANIA
BELARUS
Moscow■ ●Nizhny Novgorod
UKRAINE
Kazan●
Rostov-na-Donu ●Samara
Black Sea
Ural Mountains
R U S S I A
S I B E R I A
Arctic Circle
●Yekaterinburg
Chelyabinsk●
●Omsk
●Novosibirsk
●Khabarovsk
GEORGIA
ARMENIA *Caspian Sea* KAZAKHSTAN
AZERBAIJAN *Aral Sea*
MONGOLIA
CHINA
NORTH KOREA
JAPAN

Resources

Russia has major deposits of oil, natural gas, and coal. Siberia is rich in coal, petroleum, natural gas, diamonds, iron ore, and gold. However, the harsh climate and huge distances make it very difficult to take advantage of these **natural resources**.

Cellulose, taken from trees, is produced in Siberia, where there is a lot of timber available. Cellulose is used to make paper.

Industry

There is a wide variety of industry in Russia, because of the natural resources available. For example, chemical industries have set up around the petroleum- and gas-producing areas in the Volga-Ural zone and the North Caucasus, and in areas served by **pipelines**. Electronic equipment, such as home appliances, is manufactured in areas where there are skilled workers, mainly in and around Moscow and St. Petersburg.

Wildlife: Protecting Habitats

The plant and animal life in Russia varies depending on the landscape and climate. The tundra along northernmost Russia is frozen for most of the year. Only mosses, lichens, and grasses grow here. Animals such as reindeer, Arctic foxes, and musk oxen can also be found. In the taiga there are woodland animals such as squirrel, marten, fox, ermine, and sable. Elks, bears, muskrats, and wolves also make these forests their home. Marmots, skunks, foxes, and wolves live on the vast grasslands, called the steppes.

This herd of reindeer is looking for food under the snow near the Ural Mountains.

Russia's Lake Baikal has more than 1,700 **species** of plant and animal. About two thirds of these cannot be found anywhere else on Earth! A fish called golomyanka is unique to the lake. Unlike most fish, it gives birth to live young.

Climate change

Russia is the third biggest producer of **greenhouse gases**, after the United States and China. There are a lot of old industrial plants that pollute the environment. The process of extracting coal, oil, and petroleum causes further pollution. Greenhouse gases are the main cause of global warming and climate change. Russia is now working to reduce the emission of greenhouse gases.

National parks and protected areas

Russia has a problem with environmental pollution, so many areas are protected under the country's nature reserve system. These protected areas are known as *zapovedniks* (zap-o-ved-niks). The first *zapovednik*, called Barguzinsky, was created in 1916 on the eastern shore of Lake Baikal. There are now 101 *zapovedniks* and 37 national parks. Altogether, more than 193,000 square miles (500,000 square kilometers) of land are protected.

This mountain lake is in the Altai Mountains region of Russia. The mountains run through Russia, China, Mongolia, and Kazakhstan.

Siberian tigers facing extinction

In the 1940s, the Siberian or Amur tiger was nearly **extinct**. There were no more than 40 Siberian tigers living in the wild. Most Siberian tigers are found in Russia, but there are also some in China. Russia has made a great effort to increase the number of tigers living in the wild by trying to stop **poaching**. In 2008, Russia created two new national parks to help protect the habitat of these rare tigers. The parks are in Primorsky Krai in the far east of Russia.

Now there are around 450 individual tigers living in the wild, but they are still under threat because of continued poaching, increased **logging**, the building of new roads, and forest fires. The Cold War protected the Siberian tiger from hunting, as the areas where they lived were closed to most people. However, the collapse of the **USSR** led to a big increase in poaching, as people tried to make money by supplying tiger parts for use in traditional Chinese medicines.

The Siberian tiger is still at risk, but efforts are being made to protect it.

In October 2010, the Siberian tigers' habitat was put under threat again. The forest administration of Primorsky Province in the far east of Russia announced that there would be an **auction** for logging rights in major tiger areas. The strong public outcry, both in Russia and from the rest of the world, stopped the auction from going ahead.

YOUNG PEOPLE

In November 2010, the **WWF** Tiger Youth Forum in Vladivostok had a video conference with the prime ministers of their countries, who were attending the International Tiger Conservation Forum in St. Petersburg. The young people asked them to try to double the wild tiger population by 2022. The Tiger Youth Forum is an international group working to protect tigers.

How to say...

bear	медведь	(myed-vyed)
fox	лиса	(leeh-sah)
reindeer	северный елень	(alen-sye-ver-nyyh ah-lehn)
squirrel	белка	(byel-kah)
wolf	волк	(volk)
mountain	гора	(gah-rah)
forest	лес	(lyes)

Infrastructure: What Makes Russia Work?

A country's infrastructure is the set of systems and services that are needed for everyday life to run properly. The infrastructure includes transportation systems, schools, and hospitals. The Russian government runs the country.

Russia's full name is the Russian Federation. Being a federation means that the country is made up of regions that are partly self-governing, but also united by a central government. In the Russian Federation there are 83 administrative divisions, which include 21 republics. The republics have the right to have their own official language and have their own **constitution**.

This political map shows the different types of administrative division that make up the Russian Federation.

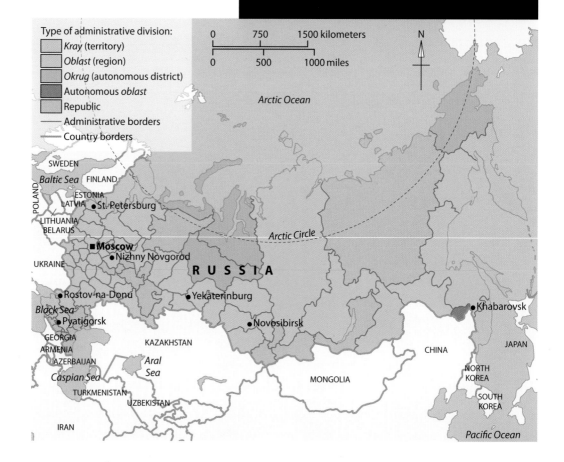

Type of administrative division:
- *Kray* (territory)
- *Oblast* (region)
- *Okrug* (autonomous district)
- Autonomous *oblast*
- Republic
- Administrative borders
- Country borders

| 0 | 750 | 1500 kilometers | N |
| 0 | 500 | 1000 miles | |

Arctic Ocean

SWEDEN
Baltic Sea FINLAND
ESTONIA
LATVIA ●St. Petersburg
LITHUANIA
BELARUS
Arctic Circle
POLAND

■**Moscow**
●Nizhny Novgorod
UKRAINE
R U S S I A

●Rostov-na-Donu ●Yekaterinburg
Black Sea
●Pyatigorsk ●Khabarovsk
●Novosibirsk
GEORGIA
KAZAKHSTAN
ARMENIA JAPAN
AZERBAIJAN *Aral* CHINA
Sea
Caspian Sea NORTH
KOREA
TURKMENISTAN MONGOLIA
UZBEKISTAN SOUTH
KOREA
IRAN
Pacific Ocean

Economic conditions

There have been major changes in the Russian **economy** since 1991. Before then Russia was part of the USSR, and its economy was cut off from most of the world. Now the economy is part of the world economy. Russia exports a lot of goods to the rest of the world, so it can be affected if the price other countries will pay for these goods goes up or down. For example, when the price of oil dropped around the world in 2008–2009, the Russian economy was badly affected.

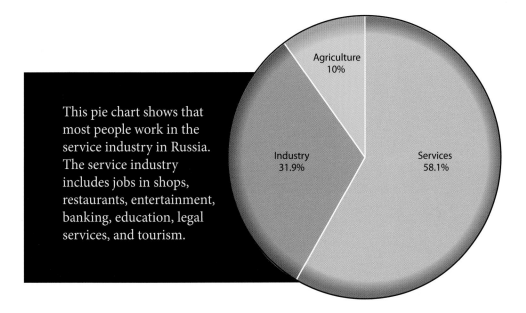

This pie chart shows that most people work in the service industry in Russia. The service industry includes jobs in shops, restaurants, entertainment, banking, education, legal services, and tourism.

Agriculture
10%

Industry
31.9%

Services
58.1%

Communications

Under the Soviet Union the government controlled all means of communication. The telephone system was used by the state to send military and government messages, rather than by ordinary people. Since 1991, there has been a great change in the telephone system in Russia. Now there is Internet access and increased use of e-mail.

Transportation

Russia relies on railways to cover its vast areas. Most of Russia's freight (goods) and about half of Russia's passengers travel by rail. There are more railway networks in some areas than others. The railways are controlled by the state.

Russia does have highways that link the major cities, but in general the road system is not very developed. The number of Russians owning a car is still small. In 2008, around 20 percent of Russians owned a car. In the United States it is around 80 percent.

Air transportation is becoming more important in Russia. Not much freight is carried by airplane, except for expensive items that need to go to and from remote parts of Siberia. Sometimes airplanes are the only means of transportation here.

The railway is an important way for people to travel around Russia.

Housing

During the time of the Soviet Union, nearly all houses were owned by the state. Private property was banned in **urban** areas, and the size of private homes was controlled in **rural** areas. In urban areas, most people lived in high-rise apartment buildings. Rents were kept very low and in most cases did not cover maintenance costs. Many apartment buildings are now in a bad state of repair. The government is supporting new home-building plans, and old buildings are being pulled down.

Daily life

In the Soviet era many people in Moscow lived in **communal** apartments called *communalki*. These apartments had kitchens and bathrooms that had to be shared among a number of families. Now many people in Moscow want to live in new homes, where they do not have to share facilties.

Health care

Basic health care is free to most of the population. However, public health care has deteriorated since the Soviet era. This is partly due to lack of funding, medicine shortages, and lack of properly trained medical staff. The government has made it a priority to improve health care. Some of the measures they want to pursue include the training or retraining of doctors, increasing wages, purchasing more equipment, and increasing **immunizations**. Russia is facing one of the fastest growing epidemics of HIV/AIDS in the world. The number of cases of people dying from tuberculosis is also high, and could be improved with an immunization program.

Education

Many children in Russia go to nursery or preschool, but it is not **compulsory**. Free, compulsory education starts when a child is seven years old. Children must go to school for at least eight years to gain a basic general education certificate. To get the secondary-level certificate, children must spend an additional two or three years at school. Many children go on to higher education. There are more than 8.5 million students in higher education.

School starts at about 8:00 a.m and finishes at 1:00 or 2:00 p.m. Children can take part in after-school activities such as dancing, sports, singing, or painting. School runs from Monday through Friday, and children either walk to school or take public transportation. Most children buy hot school lunches, rather than bringing their own from home. At school, children learn subjects such as Russian, mathematics, social sciences, humanities, and the arts.

Most Russian schools do not have a uniform. These children go to a small school in an Arctic village.

Lessons are taught in Russian, but non-Russian children are taught in their own language. Russian is compulsory at secondary school.

How to say...

book	книга	(knee-gah)
class	класс	(klahss)
school	школа	(shkoh-lah)
language	язык	(yah-zyk)
lunch	обед	(ah-byed)
teacher	учитель	(ooh-chee-tel)

Culture: Myths, Tradition, and Revival

Russia has no official religion. Before **communism**, the Russian Orthodox Church played a major part in Russian culture, and there has been a return to it now. Islam is the second largest religion in Russia. This dates back to when Russia was controlled by the Muslim Tatars in the 1200s.

Festivals and holidays

New Year is a big celebration in Russia because under the communists people were not allowed to celebrate religious festivals. New Year became the new way of celebrating Christmas. Now, since the majority of people in Russia are Christian, Christmas and Easter are also important occasions.

Daily life

One special occasion is *Maslenitsa*, or Pancake Week. This is a week of feasting before Lent to mark the end of winter. There are celebrations held all over Russia, and of course pancakes are eaten!

These Russian girls are performing a dance during the celebrations of *Maslenitsa*. They are wearing traditional Russian clothing.

Art

A famous Russian artist is the goldsmith and jeweler Karl Fabergé. He is well known for his highly decorative enamel Easter eggs made for the Russian royal family. Vasily Kandinsky is another very famous Russian artist. He was one of the leading figures in **abstract art**, and his work can be seen around the world.

Some of the world's most famous museums are found in Moscow and St. Petersburg. For example, the Pushkin Fine Arts Museum and the Hermitage in St. Petersburg.

The Kremlin in Moscow used to be the home of the Russian president and the center of communist power. Now it contains some important museums. The Kremlin building is a work of art in its own right.

Literature

There are many famous Russian poets and novelists throughout history. Two well-respected authors are Fyodor Dostoevsky and Leo Tolstoy. Dostoevsky wrote *Crime and Punishment* in 1866. Tolstoy is best known for his novels *War and Peace* (1865–1869) and *Anna Karenina* (1875–1877). Anton Chekhov is a famous Russian playwright. He wrote plays such as *The Seagull* (1896) and *The Cherry Orchard* (1904). Aleksandr Pushkin is thought by many to be one of Russia's greatest poets, novelists, and playwrights. His famous works include *Eugene Onegin* (1833) and *Boris Godunov* (1831).

Leo Tolstoy is often thought of as one of the world's greatest novelists. He was born in 1828 and died in 1910.

Music

Piotr Illyich Tchaikovsky (1840–1893) is Russia's most famous composer. He is probably best known for his 1812 overture, as well as for composing music for ballets. Another famous Russian compser was Nikolay Rimsky-Korsakov (1844–1908), who wrote "The Flight of the Bumblebee."

Russian ballet

Russia is well known for its ballet. The first ballet school was opened in
1734. In 1847 a French dancer and **choreographer** named Marius Petipa
established St. Petersburg as a center for the best ballet dancers and
choreographers. Petipa worked with the Russian Imperial Ballet for nearly
60 years on many famous ballets, including *Swan Lake*, *Sleeping Beauty*, and
The Nutcracker. The music for these three ballets was written by Tchaikovsky.

In 1909, a new, inventive touring ballet company called Ballet Russe was
founded by Sergey Diaghilev. The Ballet Russe toured Europe and North and
South America.

ANNA PAVLOVA
(1881–1931)

Anna Pavlova was the most
celebrated dancer of her time.
She was born into Tsarist Russia,
which had excellent schools for
the performing arts. Anna was
accepted into the Imperial School
of Ballet in St. Petersburg in 1891.
Her talent shone through, and she
went on to tour the world.

Sports

Sports play an important part in Russian life. Many Russian sports stars have become famous all over the world, for example, tennis players Anna Kournikova and Maria Sharapova. Anna has reached number eight in the World Tennis Association rankings. Maria became the third youngest female to win at Wimbledon in 2004, when she beat defending champion Serena Williams.

Russia has also enjoyed success in gymnastics, figure skating, and ice hockey. Russian players have been particularly strong in ice hockey. As in many countries around the world, soccer is very popular. One of the most famous players is the goalkeeper Lev Yashin. He helped Russia win the gold medal in the 1956 Olympics. Yashin died in 1990, and in his honor **FIFA** established the Yashin Award for the Best Goalkeeper in 1994. Recently, Russian soccer has been helped by an investment of millions of dollars by Roman Abramovich, a Russian businessman who owns Chelsea Football (Soccer) Club in the United Kingdom.

Russia is also well known for its successful chess players. Famous Russian chess players include Alexander Alekhine, Garry Kasparov, and Vladimir Kramnik.

Daily life

There is a lack of sporting facilities and equipment in much of Russia, so many people take part in jogging, soccer, and fishing, because these sports do not need much equipment.

Food

Western-style food is popular in Russia, but the Russian traditions are still strong. One of the traditional favorites is *blini,* which are like pancakes. *Blini* can be eaten at breakfast or as part of an appetizer (*zakuski*) with **caviar** (*ikra*), sour cream, or salmon. Russians usually have their main meal at lunchtime.

Blini

Ingredients

- 2 eggs
- 1 tablespoon white sugar
- 1/3 teaspoon salt
- 1/2 cup plain flour
- 2 cups milk
- 1 tablespoon vegetable oil
- 1 tablespoon butter

What to do

1. Whisk the eggs, sugar, and salt in a medium-sized bowl.
2. Sift the flour into the bowl, and stir in the egg mixture along with the milk.
3. Mix until smooth. The batter should be thin.

Cooking the *blini*

4. Heat a frying pan over medium heat. You should ask an adult to help you.
5. Lightly oil the pan.
6. When the oil is hot, pour about 2 tablespoons of the batter into the pan.
7. Spread the batter out evenly by tilting the pan.
8. Cook until the edges look crisp and the center appears dry.
9. Slide a spatula under the blini and flip it over.
10. Cook for about 1 minute, or until lightly brown.
12. Remove the *blini* from the pan and place it onto a plate.
13. Put a little butter on top and continue to stack the *blini* until all the batter has been used.

Russia Today

Russia's **economy** went through a difficult time during the global economic crisis of 2008–2009, but the economy is recovering. Russia still faces many challenges. A lot of money is needed to improve schools, hospitals, and roads. There is still a large difference between the wealth of people living in cities and people living in **rural** areas.

In 2010, Russia and the **European Union (EU)** agreed that Russia should enter the **World Trade Organization**. This means that Russia will be able to trade more freely with other countries across the world. International companies will come to Russia to produce goods, which will create jobs for Russian people. Russian companies will have to become more competitive if they are going to succeed against international companies, but if they can, they have the chance to sell their goods all over the world.

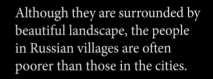

Although they are surrounded by beautiful landscape, the people in Russian villages are often poorer than those in the cities.

Russia's capital city, Moscow, has some spectacular and modern skyscrapers.

In December 2010, **FIFA** announced that Russia would be the host country for the 2018 soccer World Cup. This is the first time an eastern European country will host the event. The announcement is exciting for Russia, because it means that there will be a lot of investment in the country. In order to host the tournament, Russia will have to build 16 stadiums, a lot of hotels and airports, and hundreds of miles of roads. This will be an expensive job. It is expected that nearly $11 billion will need to be invested in the tourist industry alone. The tournament in 2018 will leave behind it some great new facilities for the Russian people to use.

Fact File

Official long name: Russian Federation

Official short name: Russia

Official language: Russian

Population: 138,739,900 (2011 estimate)

Currency: ruble

Capital city: Moscow

Area: 6,601,700 square miles (17,098,200 square kilometers)

Bordering countries: Azerbaijan, Belarus, China, Estonia, Finland, Georgia, Kazakhstan, North Korea, Latvia, Lithuania, Mongolia, Norway, Poland, Ukraine

Rivers: Russia's longest rivers are the Ob-Irtysh, Amur, Lena, and Yenisey. These rivers run through Siberia.

There are more than 100,000 rivers in Russia. The Volga is the most important river in European Russia. It is the longest river in Europe, at 2,193 miles (3,530 kilometers), and is a major trade route.

Largest lake: : Lake Ladoga— 6,700 square miles (17,350 square kilometers)

Deepest lake: Lake Baikal. Maximum depth of 5,315 feet (1,620 meters). It is the deepest and oldest existing freshwater lake on Earth and is thought to be 20 to 25 million years old.

Highest point: Mount Elbrus at 18,510 feet (5,642 meters). This is also Europe's highest peak.

Lowest point: Caspian Sea at -92 feet (-28 meters)

Temperatures: Russia has the world's lowest temperature recorded outside of Antarctica at -96 degrees Fahrenheit (-71 degrees Celsius)

Poverty rate: 13.1 percent of Russia's population live below the poverty line

Main exports: petroleum and petroleum products, natural gas, grain, wood and wood products, metals, and chemicals

Main imports: vehicles, machinery and equipment, plastics, medicines, iron and steel, consumer goods, meat, fruit and nuts, and semi-finished metal products

Main trading partners: Netherlands, Italy, Germany, China, Turkey, Ukraine, and the United States

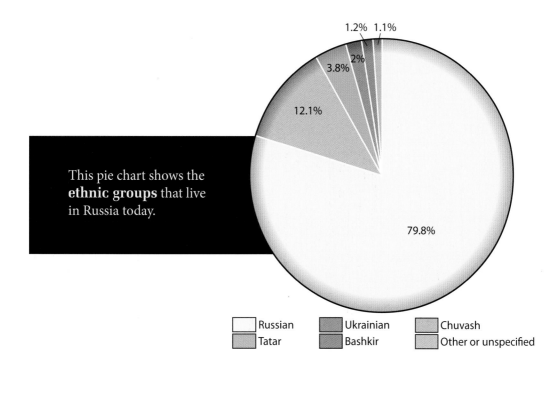

This pie chart shows the **ethnic groups** that live in Russia today.

1.2%   1.1%
2%
3.8%
12.1%
79.8%

☐ Russian   ☐ Ukrainian   ☐ Chuvash
☐ Tatar   ☐ Bashkir   ☐ Other or unspecified

Official state holidays: New Year's Day—January 1
Christmas Day—January 7
Defender of the Motherland Day—
     February 23
International Women's Day—March 8
Labor Day—May 1
Victory Day—May 9
Russia Day—June 12
National Unity Day—November 4

Christmas Day is not on December 25. This is because the Russian Orthodox Church uses a different calendar, which is 12 days behind the one used in western countries.

Famous Russians :

Tsar Peter I, called Peter the Great (1672–1725). Peter ruled from 1682 to 1725 and made Russia stronger. He made changes to the government and built a new capital city, which he called St. Petersburg.

Modest Mussorgsky (1839–1881)—composer

Konstantin Sergeyevick Stanislavsky (1863–1938)—actor, director, and producer

Sergey Prokofiev (1891–1953)—composer

Dmitry Shostakovich (1906–1975)—composer

Yury Gagarin (1934–1968)—astronaut

Rudolf Nureyev (1938–1993)—ballet dancer

Valentina Matvienko (born 1949)—governor of St. Petersburg

Vladimir Putin (born 1952)—Russia's second president in 1999–2008, and prime minister from 2008

Tatyana Golikova (born 1966)—health and social development minister in the Russian government

Andrey Arshavin (born 1981)—soccer player

Alexander Ovechkin (born 1985)—ice hockey player who played in the 2010 Winter Olympics

National anthem:

Russia's national anthem was adapted from the music of the Soviet Union's anthem, with words by Sergey Mikhalkov. Below is an English translation.

Russia—our holy nation,
Russia—our beloved country.
A mighty will, great glory—
These are yours for all time!

Chorus:
Be glorious, our free Motherland,
Age-old union of fraternal peoples,
Popular wisdom given by our forebears!
Be glorious, our country! We are proud of you!

From the southern seas to the polar lands
Spread our forests and fields.
You are unique in the world, one of a kind—
Native land protected by God!

Chorus

Wide spaces for dreams and for living
Are opened for us by the coming years
Our loyalty to our Motherland gives us strength.
Thus it was, thus it is and always will be!

Chorus

Timeline

BCE means "before the common era." When this appears after a date it refers to the number of years before the Christian religion began. BCE dates are always counted backward.

CE means "common era." When this appears after a date, it refers to the time after the Christian religion began.

862 CE	Rurik becomes leader of Russia and starts the first Russian **dynasty**
1613	Mikail Romanov is elected to rule and is the first ruler of the Romanov Dynasty
1734	The first ballet school opens in Russia
1762	The Russian army arrests Tsar Peter III
	Tsar Peter III's wife, Catherine, becomes ruler of Russia. She will later become known as Catherine the Great.
1796	Catherine the Great dies
1865–1869	Leo Tolstoy writes *War and Peace*
1866	Fyodor Dostoevsky writes *Crime and Punishment*
1875–1877	Tolstoy writes *Anna Karenina*
1896	Anton Chekov writes *The Seagull*
1905	The Russian Revolution takes place
1909	The Ballet Russe is founded
1916	The first *zapovednik* (nature reserve) is created on the eastern shore of Lake Baikal

1917	The last Russian tsar, Tsar Nicholas II, **abdicates**
	The second Russian Revolution leads to the Bolshevik Party seizing control of Russia. Lenin takes control.
1918	Bolsheviks murder tsar Nicholas II and his family
1922	The **USSR** (Union of Soviet Socialist **Republics**) is founded
1924	Lenin dies of a stroke
	Joseph Stalin seizes power of the Communist Party and the USSR. His time in power becomes known as the "Great Terror."
1932–1933	**Famine** in Ukraine kills four to five million peasants
1939	Stalin and Hitler make a secret pact not to attack each other
	Hitler invades Poland and World War II begins
1941	Germany invades the USSR, breaking Hitler's pact with Stalin
1945	Germany is defeated and World War II ends
1953	Stalin dies
1985	Mikhail Gorbachev becomes head of the Communist Party and changes the law, allowing ordinary people to speak more freely and be involved in politics
1988	Gorbachev becomes president of the USSR
1989	Eastern European countries leave the USSR
1991	The Soviet Union ends and Russia becomes an independent nation. Gorbachev resigns.
2010	**FIFA** announces that Russia will host the 2018 World Cup

Glossary

abdicate give up right to the throne

abstract art art that tries to show ideas rather than the way things look

allied forces military forces of a group of countries, including Russia, the UK, and the U.S., who fought against Germany in World War II

auction sale in which goods or property is sold to the person who bids (offers) the highest amount of money

Bolsheviks division of Social Democrats led by Lenin

caviar eggs of a large fish, eaten as a delicacy

choreographer person who plans out the steps a dance

civil war war between people of the same country

collective farm farm in which land and tools are owned by the state rather than by an individual

communal shared or done by all members of a group

communism political theory that believes in state ownership of goods for the benefit of all. A supporter of communism is called a communist.

compulsory required or demanded

democratic system of government

dictator leader who has complete power in a country and has not been elected by the people

dynasty family of rulers

economy relating to the money, industry, and jobs in a country

emperor ruler of an empire

empire group of states or countries under one ruler

ethnic group group of people sharing the same national or cultural traditions

European Union (EU) international organization of European countries with shared political and economic aims. The EU formed from the EEC (European Economic Community) in 1993.

extinct die out completely

famine large-scale lack of food over a wide area, leading to starvation

FIFA the international governing body of soccer

greenhouse gases gases, such as carbon dioxide, that trap the Sun's energy and make Earth warm up

immunization vaccination

imperial royal

industrializing make more industrial

inflation rise in prices

logging cutting and preparing forest timber

missionaries people who travel to a foreign country to do religious or charitable work

natural resource thing that exists naturally and is used by people, such as coal, oil, or forests

Nazi member of the National Socialist Party in Germany during Hitler's time

pipelines pipes that take gas or oil to where it is needed

poaching hunting and catching animals illegally

raw material natural substance that other things are made from

Red Terror mass excecutions of political opponents of Lenin

republic country with an elected government and a president instead of a king or queen

rural to do with the countryside

Slavic people people from central and eastern Europe who speak a Slavonic language, such as Russian

species category in the classification system; group of a particular type

undulating having a wavy surface or shape

United Nations (UN) international organization set up in 1945 to promote international peace

urban to do with a town or city

USSR stands for Union of Soviet Socialist Republics, also called the Soviet Union. The USSR was an empire in which communist Russia controlled neighboring countries from 1917 to 1991.

World Trade Organization international body whose aim is to get countries to trade more freely with each other by getting rid of duties and barriers

WWF charity that used to be known as the World Wildlife Fund for Nature. The WWF helps to protect endangered animals and habitats.

Find Out More

Books

Marsico, Katie. *It's Cool to Learn about Countries: Russia.* Ann Arbor, MI: Cherry Lake Publishing, 2010.

Nickles, Greg. *Russia: The Culture.* New York: Crabtree Publishing, 2008.

Nickles, Greg. *Russia: The Land.* New York: Crabtree Publishing, 2008.

Nickles, Greg. *Russia: The People.* New York: Crabtree Publishing, 2008.

Ransome, Gayla. *Russia in Our World.* Mankato, MN: Smart Apple Media, 2010.

Raum, Elizabeth. *Catherine the Great.* Chicago: Heinemann-Raintree, 2008.

Russell, Henry. *Russia.* Washington, DC: National Geographic Children's Books, 2008.

DVDs

Biography—Vladimir Lenin: Voice of Revolution. New York: A&E Home Video, 2005.

Emily Bruni, Dan Badarau, Paul Burgess, and John-Paul Davidson. *Catherine the Great.* Arlington, VA: PBS, 2006.

Families of Russia. Directed by Mark Marquisee. Cincinnati, OH: Master Communications Inc., 2006.

Ian Wright. *Globe Trekker: Russia.* London: Pilot Productions, 2004.

Russian Revolution in Color. Newton, NJ: Shanachie Entertainment, 2007.

Websites

www.wild-russia.org/default.htm

Find out more about Russian nature conservation.

kids.nationalgeographic.com/kids/places/find/russia

This website contains facts about Russia and plenty of photos. It also includes a short video about Russia's volcanoes.

www.cia.gov/library/publications/the-world-factbook/geos/rs.html

The World Factbook is a publication of the Central Intelligence Agency (CIA) of the United States. It provides information on the history, people, government, economy, geography, communications, transportation, and military of Russia and over 250 other countries.

Places to visit

If you ever get the chance to go to Russia, here are some interesting places to visit:

Red Square, Moscow
Here, you can see St. Basil's Cathedral, The Kremlin, and Lenin's Mausoleum.

Pushkin Museum of Fine Arts, Moscow
This museum contains a famous collection of Impressionist and Post-Impressionist paintings. It also has an exhibition of controversial paintings stolen from European Jews by the Nazis, which were rescued by Soviet troops.

The Hermitage, St. Petersburg
This art collection is housed in the palace from which the tsars ruled the Russian Empire.

Church of Our Savior on Spilled Blood (Spas na Kravi), St. Petersburg
This beautiful, old-style Russian church has spectacular blue-and-gold, onion-shaped domes and is filled with spectacular mosaics.

The Russian Museum, St. Petersburg
This museum has a large collection of Russian and other art held in former palace buildings.

Topic Tools

You can use these topic tools for your school projects. Trace the map onto a sheet of paper, using the black outline to guide you.

Russia's flag has three equal horizontal bands of white, blue, and red. There is no official meaning behind these colors. Copy the flag design and then color in your picture. Make sure you use the right colors!

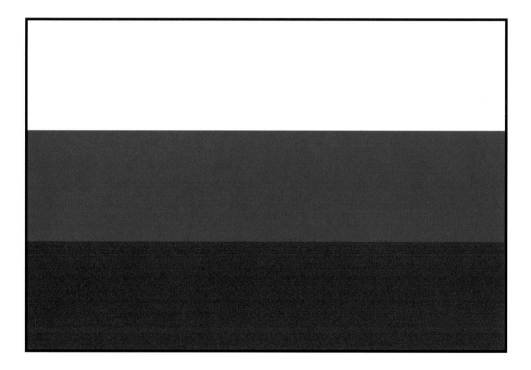

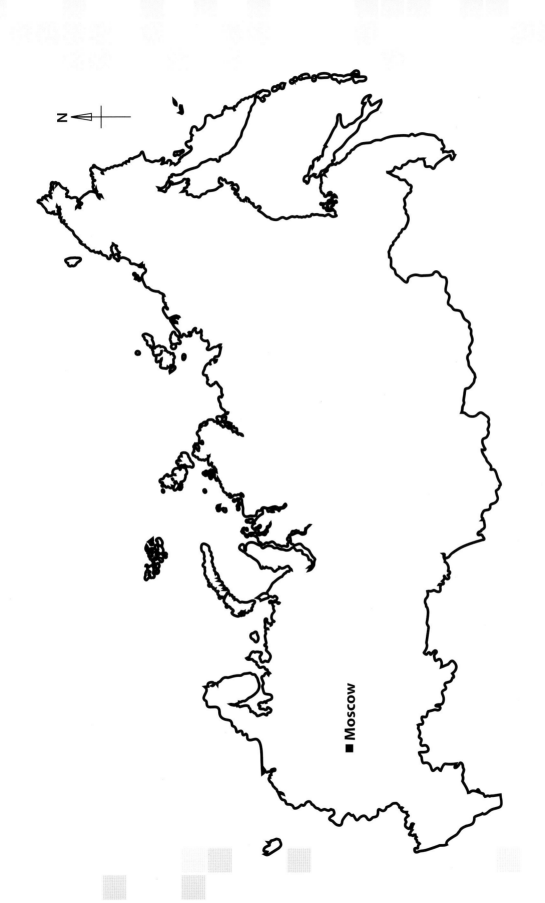

■ Moscow

Index